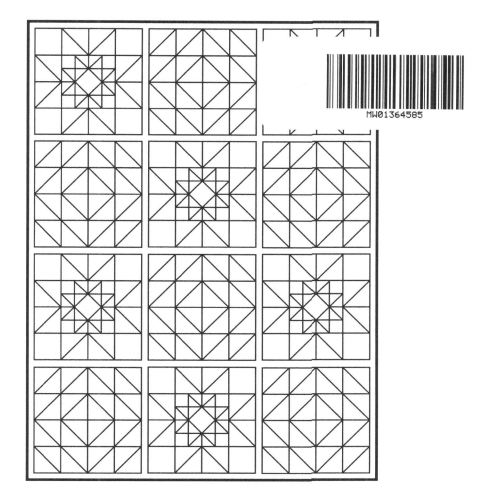

Quilting Designs Quilt
Coloring Book

By Lilt Kids Coloring Books

Copyright © 2016 by Lilt House

All rights reserved. This book or any portion thereof
may not be reproduced or used in any manner whatsoever
without the express written permission of the publisher
except for the use of brief quotations in a book review.

COLOR TEST PAGE

COLOR TEST PAGE

• COLORING TIPS •

1) Relax & Enjoy:
Coloring is good for stress relief, anxiety, depression, and so much more. There's no wrong way to color. You can do it while you watch television, listen to music, drink tea, or while you do nothing but focus on your coloring. Don't compare your finished product to anyone else's. You'll improve the longer you keep at it, and you probably won't love every single image you create. That's okay! If you are enjoying the journey, that's all that matters.

2) Choose the right tools:
Colored pencils, crayons, markers, oh my! What you choose to color with is a very personal choice. Visit LiltKids.com/tools for a rundown of our favorite brands. If you choose markers, we recommend you put a blank sheet of paper behind your page so that the colors don't run through onto the next image.

3) Color schemes:
Try out your colors in the test pages at the beginning of this book, and pick out some that might go well together. If you also google "color scheme", you will find an abundance of websites for inspiration.

4) Getting the pages out of your book:
Unfortunately, we don't yet have the ability to offer perforated pages in our books. However, you can find a tool called a page perforator on amazon.com for under $4, and turn any coloring book page into a perforated page!

5) Share your work:
We want to see what you color! So do our illustrators. Snap a photo and show us your work. Go to LiltKids.com, and click on the social media link of your choice: facebook, twitter, instagram, or pinterest.

Or email it to us and we'll share it for you!

LiltKidsColoring@gmail.com

Really, we want to see it.

We hope you enjoy this book!
If you do, please consider leaving a review on
Amazon.com, it really helps us out.

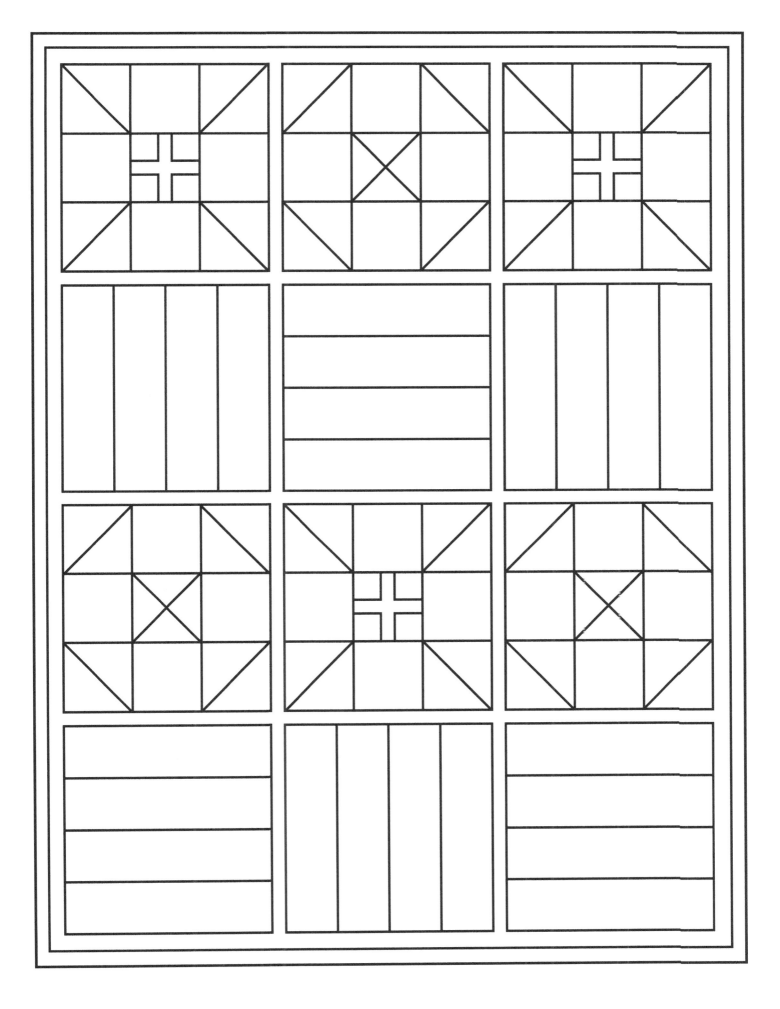

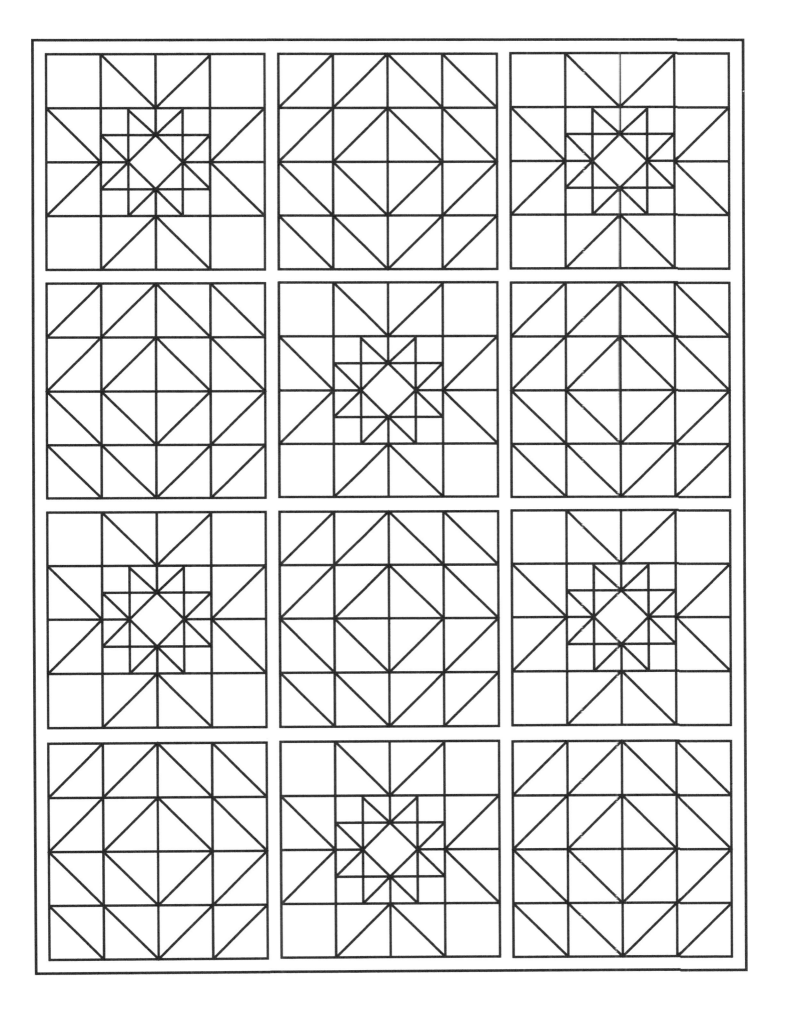

Like us on **facebook**

Are you an Adult who Likes to Color?

You've got friends!

Meet others who love to Color just like you in our online community.

Share your work or see what others are coloring.

Free coloring book giveaways!

Go to LiltKids.com and join our Facebook group or email list. Or search Facebook, Twitter, or Pinterest for "Lilt Kids".

Please Leave USA Review On Amazon!

Made in the USA
Middletown, DE
01 July 2021